PARIS
WITH KIDS

MARCIE CHEUNG

to my husband Darren and our boys Owen and Hugo,
who are always up for exploring Paris with me...as
long as there are macarons and carousels involved!

Contents

Meet Marcie

I'm Marcie, a Seattle-area family travel blogger who loves exploring top family travel destinations like Paris!

I first visited Paris on a group trip in high school with my history teacher where I somehow navigated the city (and the Metro system) without GPS or a cell phone. I've been back many times since and it's one of my favorite cities in the world.

My family travels a LOT. It's one of the perks of being a travel writer. But if you ask my kids where they'd like to go on their next trip, I guarantee they will say Paris. That's because we've done some incredible tours there and found the coolest places to go and things to do that keeps them engaged (and learning).

I launched my family travel blog Marcie in Mommyland to equip families with the knowledge and confidence to travel the world with their kids, no matter their ages. I hope this guide helps you plan your perfect Paris family getaway!

This guide may contain affiliate links.

Marcie x

Get In Touch!
marcieinmommyland@gmail.com
marcieinmommyland.com

@MarcieinMommyland

Welcome!

Paris is one of the most famous European cities to visit with your family. It's easy to weave in history lessons about the French Revolution or World War II, taste traditional croissants and macarons, see famous artwork, and so much more.

Things to know

BEFORE YOUR TRIP

Iconic Landmarks

Paris is home to iconic landmarks like the Eiffel Tower, Arc de Triomphe, and Notre Dame Cathedral.

Top Art Museums

The city is home to some of the world's best art museums, such as the Louvre and Musee d'Orsay.

Eiffel Tower

Every night, the Eiffel Tower puts on a dazzling light show that lasts for 5 minutes every hour on the hour after sunset, captivating children and adults alike with its beauty.

Science Museum

Paris is home to the largest science museum in Europe. The Cité des Sciences et de l'Industrie is a hit with curious minds, featuring interactive exhibits on science and technology, including a planetarium and a submarine.

Disneyland Paris

Just a short train ride away from the city center, Disneyland Paris offers magical experiences for families, with rides, parades, and encounters with beloved Disney characters.

Top 5 Questions

I'm sure you have a lot of questions about planning a trip to Paris with kids, so here are a few answers right off the bat.

What's the best time of year to visit Paris with kids?

If possible, Spring (April to June) and Fall (September to October) are the best times to visit as the weather is pleasant, it's more affordable, and the crowds are smaller than in summer. However, our family loves to visit Paris during the summer months.

What are the must-visit attractions in Paris?

The Eiffel Tower, Luxembourg Gardens, Cité des Sciences et de l'Industrie, Disneyland Paris, and Jardin d'Acclimatation are great for kids.

Where should I stay in Paris with kids?

Paris offers numerous family-friendly hotels and apartments. Look for accommodations in central areas like the Marais or near Luxembourg Gardens for close proximity to playgrounds and attractions. Our family really likes Hotel Edgar but we also recommend Roi de Sicile, Hôtel du Levant, and Hôtel Central Saint Germain.

What are the best kid-friendly restaurants in Paris?

Paris has many cafes and restaurants offering children's menus. Bakeries and creperies are also hits with young visitors. Our family likes Chez Andre and Le Relais de l'Entrecôte.

Should I bring a stroller to Paris?

Most major sites and public transport are stroller-friendly, though some Metro stations lack elevators. The cobblestone streets can be tricky, so make sure you have a sturdy stroller.

Where to stay with kids

Where to Stay

When visiting Paris with your family, picking the right neighborhood to stay in can make your trip extra special. A few of the most popular areas include Le Marais, Luxembourg Gardens, and the Latin Quarter.

Questions to Help You Decide:

Answering these questions will help you determine the smartest place to stay.

WHAT DO WE WANT TO DO IN PARIS?

Think about if you want to be close to specific attractions or parks.

DO WE LIKE BUSY PLACES OR QUIET SPOTS?

Some neighborhoods are more lively and bustling, while others offer a more relaxed vibe.

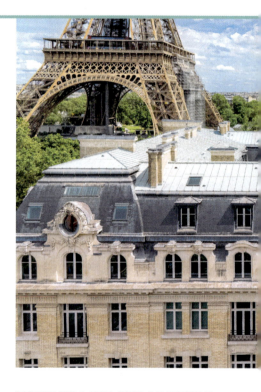

HOW WILL WE GET AROUND?

Consider if you prefer walking to most places or if you're okay with taking public transport.

WHAT'S OUR BUDGET?

Some areas might be pricier than others, so think about how much you want to spend.

Le Marais

This historic area is super cool because it has a mix of old and new. It's like traveling back in time with its beautiful old buildings, but it also has lots of trendy shops and yummy places to eat. Le Marais is great for families who love to explore on foot, discover cool shops, and eat delicious food.

Hôtel Les Jardins du Marais

📍 74 Rue Amelot, 75011

📞 33 1 40 21 20 00

This hotel boasts spacious suites that are perfect for families needing extra room. Its beautiful private gardens provide a rare green space in the heart of Paris, ideal for children to play and parents to relax.

Le Pavillon de la Reine

📍 28 Pl. des Vosges, 75003 Paris

📞 33 1 40 29 19 19

Situated on the picturesque Place des Vosges, this hotel offers luxury family rooms and complimentary amenities for young children. Its quiet location and beautiful courtyard make it a peaceful retreat after a busy day of exploring.

Hôtel de la Bretonnerie

📍 22 Rue Sainte-Croix de la Bretonnerie, 75004

📞 33 1 48 87 77 63

A charming option for families, this hotel has family rooms decorated in a cozy, traditional Parisian style. It's within walking distance to many attractions and parks, making it convenient for sightseeing with kids.

Hôtel Caron de Beaumarchais

⭐⭐⭐⭐⭐

📍 12 Rue Vieille du Temple, 75004

📞 33 1 42 72 34 12

Offering a musical and 18th-century literary theme, this hotel captivates with its unique decor and friendly atmosphere. The location is fantastic for exploring Le Marais, and the staff is known for being especially attentive to families.

Hôtel Emile

⭐⭐⭐⭐⭐

📍 2 Rue Malher, 75004

📞 33 1 42 72 76 16

With its modern design and comfortable family rooms, Hôtel Emile is a great option for those seeking a more contemporary stay. Its central location in Le Marais means easy access to cafes, shops, and playgrounds that are fun for kids.

Luxembourg Garden

The area around Luxembourg Garden, also known as the 6th arrondissement of Paris, is one of the city's most charming and family-friendly neighborhoods. It's an ideal place for families who want a mix of outdoor activities, culture, and relaxation in a setting that feels quintessentially Parisian. Plus, its central location means you're never too far from other major attractions in Paris.

Hôtel Les Jardins du Luxembourg

📍 5 Imp. Royer-Collard, 75005

📞 33 1 40 46 08 88

Offering views that overlook the garden itself, this beautiful hotel is ideal for families who want to be as close as possible to a large, safe space for their children to play. The hotel's comfortable family rooms and complimentary breakfast make it a hit with traveling families.

Hôtel Le Clos Medicis

📍 56 Rue Monsieur le Prince, 75006

📞 33 1 43 29 10 80

Just a short walk from Luxembourg Garden, Hôtel Le Clos Medicis offers cozy rooms in a historic setting. The hotel's quiet courtyard is perfect for families looking to unwind after a day of sightseeing, and the proximity to the garden means easy access to one of Paris's best playgrounds.

Hôtel Saint-Paul RiveGauche

📍 43 Rue Monsieur le Prince, 75006

📞 33 1 43 26 98 64

Nestled in a 17th-century building, this hotel combines charm with family-friendly amenities, including connecting rooms for larger families. Its central location, close to Luxembourg Garden, makes it an excellent choice for those looking to explore Paris on foot with kids.

Hotel Observatoire Luxembourg

📍 107 Bd Saint-Michel, 75005

📞 33 1 46 34 10 12

This boutique hotel features family suites with bunk beds for kids, making it a fun and practical choice for accommodations. Its location across from Luxembourg RER station provides easy access to wider Paris, and the garden is just a stone's throw away for leisurely afternoons.

Hotel Edgar

📍 1 Rue Sainte-Foy, 75002

📞 33 1 40 41 05 19

You'll love the spacious family rooms, which offer a comfortable and convenient base for families exploring Paris. There's also a great restaurant downstairs with kid-friendly options.

Latin Quarter

This neighborhood is known for its lively atmosphere and historic sites. It's close to the Notre-Dame Cathedral (which is being rebuilt) and the beautiful Luxembourg Gardens, where kids can play and you can relax. There are also lots of bookshops and cafes. The Latin Quarter is great for families who want to enjoy famous sights and Paris's beautiful parks.

Hotel Les Bulles De Paris

📍 32 Rue des Écoles, 75005

📞 33 1 46 34 12 90

Celebrating the joy of champagne, this unique hotel offers a playful yet elegant atmosphere that can be a hit with parents. It is also sophisticated enough to ensure a comfortable stay. Family rooms are available, and its location makes it easy to explore the Latin Quarter and nearby attractions like the Luxembourg Gardens.

Hotel Saint Jacques

📍 35 Rue des Écoles, 75005

📞 33 1 44 07 45 45

Offering classic Parisian charm, Hotel Saint Jacques provides spacious family rooms decorated in a Belle Époque style, making it a cozy retreat for families. Its central location in the Latin Quarter is perfect for visiting nearby sights like the Panthéon and Notre Dame Cathedral.

Familia Hotel

📍 11 Rue des Écoles, 75005

📞 33 1 43 54 55 27

As the name suggests, Familia Hotel focuses on welcoming families, offering themed rooms that can captivate children and adults alike. The hotel provides modern amenities within walking distance to the Jardin des Plantes, a great spot for families to explore.ractions and parks, making it convenient for sightseeing with kids.

Hotel Minerve

★★★★★

📍 13 Rue des Écoles, 75005

📞 33 1 43 26 26 04

Set in a 19th-century Haussmannian building, Hotel Minerve offers comfortable and stylish accommodation, including family rooms. Its location near the Seine and Notre Dame provides a picturesque base from which to explore the heart of Paris, with plenty of kid-friendly activities and dining options nearby.

Hotel La Lanterne

★★★★★

📍 12 Rue de la Montagne Ste Geneviève, 75005

📞 33 1 53 19 88 39

A boutique hotel with a blend of modern and traditional design, Hotel La Lanterne offers an indoor pool – a rare find in Paris – which can be a big hit with kids after a day of sightseeing. It is situated close to the Luxembourg Gardens and provides a peaceful yet central location for families exploring the city.

Eating
in Paris

Restaurants for Families

Dining in Paris with children can be a delightful experience, offering a chance to indulge in the city's renowned culinary scene while embracing family-friendly dining culture. Here are a few key points and tips parents should know about navigating restaurants in Paris:

THINGS PARENTS SHOULD KNOW:

Early Dining: Unlike some Parisians who dine late, families are often seated earlier, around 6:00 to 7:30 PM. Not all restaurants are open throughout the day, so try to plan meals around French dining hours.

Kids' Menus: While not as common as in other countries, some restaurants do offer kids' menus ("menu enfant"). These menus are usually simpler and cater to younger palates.

Welcoming Atmosphere: Many Parisian restaurants are welcoming to families, but it's always a good idea to check if the restaurant you're interested in is kid-friendly. Look for places with a relaxed atmosphere where a little noise won't disrupt the ambiance.

Outdoor Seating: Many Parisian restaurants and cafes have outdoor seating, which can be more spacious and less formal, making it a great option for families wanting to enjoy a meal without worrying about disturbing other diners.

High Chairs and Facilities: Not all restaurants in Paris have high chairs or changing facilities available. If these are essential for your family, it's worth checking in advance or choosing more family-oriented or larger restaurants where such amenities are more common.

HELPFUL TIPS

Reservations: For popular restaurants, making a reservation is recommended, especially for dinner. This ensures you have a table and can help the restaurant prepare for any special requests, such as a high chair.

Carry Snacks: With the time between meals and the pace of service slower than some are accustomed to, having snacks on hand for young children can help keep hunger at bay while waiting for your meal.

Embrace Local Cuisine: Use dining out as an opportunity to introduce your children to French cuisine. Many dishes, such as crepes, baguettes, and cheese, are often loved by kids.

Picnics: For a more relaxed meal, consider picking up food from a local market or boulangerie and having a picnic in one of Paris's beautiful parks. It's a fun and stress-free dining option that children usually enjoy.

Restaurants

Coffee

Caféothèque: Located near the Seine, this cozy coffee shop offers a relaxed atmosphere and a selection of beans from around the world, perfect for starting your day in Paris.

Strada Café: With locations in the Latin Quarter and Marais, Strada Café offers a cozy atmosphere perfect for families to enjoy a cup of coffee or a light snack.

Coutume Café: A spacious coffee shop that roasts its own beans, Coutume is great for parents looking for a caffeine fix and offers space for kids to be more at ease.

Breakfast

Holybelly 5: Known for its hearty breakfasts and brunches that combine French ingredients with international flavors, it's a hit with families. Be prepared for a wait, but it's worth it!

Eggs&Co: Specializing in breakfast all day, Eggs&Co offers a variety of egg dishes and pancakes, making it a hit with families.

Café de la Paix: Offering a luxurious breakfast experience near the Opéra Garnier, this historic café is a treat for families looking for a special start to their day.

Patisseries

Pierre Hermé: Renowned for inventive flavors of macarons, this patisserie is a must-visit for families with a sweet tooth. The Ispahan macaron is a crowd-pleaser.

Angelina: Famous for its decadent hot chocolate and Mont-Blanc pastry, Angelina offers a luxurious break from sightseeing, with a beautiful Belle Époque tearoom.

Ladurée: Famous for its macarons and elegant tea rooms, Ladurée is a Parisian institution that offers a delightful experience for families.

Cafes

Le Consulat: Located in the heart of Montmartre, this café offers a glimpse into Parisian life with a simple yet delicious menu, making it a great spot for a light lunch or snack.

Café de Flore: One of the oldest and most prestigious coffeehouses in Paris, it's a bit pricey but offers the quintessential Parisian café experience. The hot chocolate is beloved by kids.

Café des Deux Moulins: Made famous by the film Amélie, this café in Montmartre offers a charming setting for families to enjoy a meal or a snack.

Dinner

Bouillon Pigalle: Offering traditional French dishes at affordable prices, this bustling spot is great for families wanting to sample classic Parisian cuisine without breaking the bank.

Le Relais de l'Entrecôte: Known for its simple menu featuring salad, steak, and fries, served with its famous secret sauce, it's a hit with families. No reservations needed, but there may be a line.

Pizzeria Popolare: Part of the Big Mamma group, this lively Italian restaurant serves up delicious pizzas, pasta, and more in a fun and family-friendly atmosphere.

Kid-Friendly Activities

Babies & Toddlers

YES, THERE ARE PLENTY OF THINGS TO DO WHEN VISITING PARIS WITH A BABY OR TODDLER.

ACTIVITIES

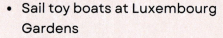

- Sail toy boats at Luxembourg Gardens
- Ride one of the many carousels around the city
- Take the little blue train around Montmartre
- Explore Jardin d'Acclimatation. This amusement park is ideal for toddlers, featuring gentle rides, a petting zoo, and a variety of play areas.
- A boat cruise along the Seine is a perfect way to see many of Paris's most famous sights without tiring little legs. Many companies offer family-friendly cruises with commentary that will interest both adults and children.
- Located in the Trocadéro Gardens, the Aquarium de Paris isn't just about marine life; it also offers touch pools, films, and workshops that are suitable for young children.

BEST MUSEUMS & ATTRACTIONS FOR LITTLE ONES

CITÉ DES ENFANTS AT CITÉ DES SCIENCES ET DE L'INDUSTRIE

Specifically designed for kids, this interactive museum offers two areas: one for 2-7-year-olds and another for 5-12-year-olds. It's a hands-on museum where little ones can explore, play, and learn.

MUSÉUM NATIONAL D'HISTOIRE NATURELLE

Located in the Jardin des Plantes, this museum complex includes the Grande Galerie de l'Evolution, the Menagerie (a small zoo), and themed gardens that are perfect for exploring.

MUSÉE EN HERBE

An art museum for children, Musée en Herbe presents exhibitions and workshops that introduce young visitors to art in a fun and accessible way. It's engaging for toddlers, thanks to its interactive displays and activities.

Ages 5-10

YOU WON'T HAVE A PROBLEM FINDING INTERESTING THINGS TO DO IN PARIS WITH SCHOOL-AGE KIDS.

Jardin d'Acclimatation

This amusement park has been delighting children since 1860. It offers a range of attractions, from puppet shows and pony rides to more modern rides suitable for this age group.

Luxembourg Gardens

With its famous Guignol puppet shows, vintage carousel, and large playground, it's a perfect spot for children to play and explore. Sailing small boats in the garden's pond is a classic Parisian pastime.

Seine River Cruise

A boat tour on the Seine is an excellent way for kids to see many of Paris's iconic sights from a unique perspective. Many companies offer commentary specifically tailored to younger audiences.

Eiffel Tower

Climbing the Eiffel Tower can be an adventure, with the option to take the stairs to the first or second level. The view from the top is always a hit with kids, offering a bird's eye view of Paris.

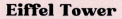

PARC DE LA VILLETTE

This park not only houses the Cité des Sciences et de l'Industrie but also offers wide-open spaces for playing, thematic gardens, and the Dragon Slide, one of the longest slides in Paris.

WORKSHOPS AND CLASSES

Many museums and cultural sites offer workshops and classes for children, from art workshops at the Louvre to cooking classes designed for young chefs.

TREASURE HUNT AT MONTMARTRE

Exploring Montmartre through a treasure hunt allows kids to discover the history and secrets of this bohemian neighborhood in a fun way.

BEST MUSEUMS & ATTRACTIONS FOR SCHOOL AGE CHILDREN

CITÉ DES SCIENCES ET DE L'INDUSTRIE

This is Europe's largest science museum, featuring interactive exhibits on science and technology, including a planetarium, a submarine, and the Cité des Enfants, an area specifically designed for kids.

MUSÉUM NATIONAL D'HISTOIRE NATURELLE

Kids can marvel at dinosaur skeletons, mineral displays, and a variety of taxidermy animals. The Gallery of Evolution, and the small zoo, La Ménagerie, in the Jardin des Plantes is perfect for age.

MUSÉE DE LA MAGIE

This magic museum is a wonderland for children, with its collection of magical artifacts and live magic shows. It offers a fascinating look into the history of magic and illusions.

PALAIS DE LA DÉCOUVERTE

This interactive science museum offers hands-on exhibits in physics, astronomy, and more, making science fun and accessible. The planetarium is a highlight.

LOUVRE MUSEUM

While it might seem ambitious, the Louvre can be fascinating for kids, especially with themed tours and trails designed for families, such as the "Egyptian Antiquities" or "Adventures at the Museum" trail.

Tweens & Teens

THIS CAN BE A TRICKY AGE FOR FAMILY TRAVEL, BUT PARIS HAS TONS OF OPTIONS THAT WILL INTEREST EVEN THE TOUGHEST-TO-PLEASE.

CATACOMBS OF PARIS

For an adventurous and slightly eerie experience, the Catacombs offer a unique glimpse into Paris's history. The underground tunnels, lined with the remains of millions of Parisians, tell a fascinating story of the city's past.

STREET ART TOUR

Explore Paris's vibrant street art scene with a guided tour of neighborhoods like Belleville and the 13th arrondissement. It's a great way to see a different side of Parisian culture and art.

ESCAPE GAMES

Paris offers numerous escape rooms, which are a fun challenge for families. Themes range from historical to fantastical, providing an engaging activity that requires teamwork and problem-solving.

SEINE RIVER CRUISE AT NIGHT

Seeing Paris's monuments illuminated at night from a boat on the Seine can be a magical experience. Teens appreciate the romantic and picturesque views of the city's landmarks.

BIKING TOUR

Join a guided biking tour or rent bikes to explore the Paris's streets, parks, and riverbanks. It's an active and eco-friendly way to see the city that will appeal to your teens' desire for independence, adventure and a bit of freedom, while still being under your watchful eye.

VISIT MONTMARTRE

This artistic neighborhood, with its street artists, cafes, and the Sacré-Cœur Basilica, offers a bohemian vibe that many teens find appealing. The view of Paris from the basilica is also a highlight.

SHOPPING IN LE MARAIS

For teens interested in fashion, Le Marais offers a mix of trendy boutiques, vintage shops, and flagship stores. It's a great area for exploring Parisian style and picking up unique finds.

BEST MUSEUMS & ATTRACTIONS FOR TWEENS & TEENS

LOUVRE MUSEUM

Beyond being home to the Mona Lisa, the Louvre offers treasure hunts and themed trails, making the exploration of art history interactive and fun. Teens interested in history and art will find the ancient civilizations sections particularly fascinating.

MUSÉE D'ORSAY

With its impressive collection of Impressionist and Post-Impressionist masterpieces, the Musée d'Orsay can captivate teens with its vivid artworks and the stories behind them. The museum's architecture, a former railway station, is also impressive.

PALAIS DE TOKYO

For families interested in contemporary art and culture, Palais de Tokyo offers an edgy and sometimes provocative look at modern artistic expression. Its dynamic exhibitions and installations encourage reflection and discussion.

CITÉ DES SCIENCES ET DE L'INDUSTRIE

This science museum appeals to curious minds with exhibits on space, technology, and the environment. The interactive displays and the planetarium are particularly popular with tweens and teens.

FOUNDATION LOUIS VUITTON

Showcasing modern and contemporary art, the foundation is housed in an architecturally stunning building designed by Frank Gehry. The exhibitions appeal to a younger audience.

Must-Visit Playgrounds

1

Le Jardin du Luxembourg

This historic garden has a large playground with slides, swings, and climbing frames, plus pony rides and puppet shows, making it a favorite among families (including ours!).

2

Parc de la Villette Playground

Located in one of Paris's largest parks, this amazing playground features giant wooden dragons, slides, and climbing structures, appealing to adventurous kids.

3

Jardin d'Acclimatation

More than just a playground, this amusement park offers rides, animal encounters, and a variety of play areas tailored to different age groups.

4

Parc des Buttes-Chaumont

Known for its beautiful landscape, the park also has a great playground with slides, swings, and a carousel, plus plenty of space for picnics.

5

Jardin des Tuileries

Close to the Louvre, this historic garden has a playground, trampolines, and a seasonal ferris wheel, providing fun against a picturesque backdrop.

6

Parc Monceau

This elegant park features classic playground equipment, a carousel, and beautiful walking paths, making it a peaceful escape in the city.

7

Jardin des Plantes

Along with its renowned botanical collections, the garden offers a small zoo and playground areas, perfect for a day of educational and physical activity.

Tips for Visiting Paris with a Baby or Toddler

We visited Paris with both babies and toddlers, and we were pleasantly surprised by how accommodating the people were. We had strangers who helped us with strollers up and down the Metro stairs and restaurant hosts who added an extra table and chairs so our hangry toddler could eat.

Here are some honest and helpful tips for parents planning a trip to Paris with little ones.

ACCOMMODATION CHOICES

Choose a centrally located hotel or apartment to minimize travel time and make naptime more manageable. Having a fridge or kitchenette can be invaluable for preparing snacks and meals.

STROLLER ACCESSIBILITY

While Paris is relatively stroller-friendly, some areas, especially older Metro stations, may lack elevators or escalators. Lightweight strollers or baby carriers can make navigating the city easier. I'd also avoid bringing a double stroller, if at all possible.

PUBLIC TRANSPORTATION

Buses in Paris are more stroller-friendly compared to the Metro. Plan routes that minimize changes, and avoid rush hours to ensure a more comfortable ride.

CHANGING FACILITIES

Larger public attractions and department stores usually have baby-changing facilities, but smaller cafes or restaurants might not. It's helpful to bring a portable changing mat.

FEEDING

Breastfeeding in public is generally accepted, but discretion is appreciated. Many cafes and restaurants are accommodating, but space might be cramped. Consider scouting a quiet spot in one of Paris's beautiful parks for nursing or breaks.

QUIET TIMES

Paris is bustling and vibrant, which can be overwhelming for little ones. Schedule some quiet time away from the crowds, such as visiting one of the city's many parks or gardens. You can also time a sightseeing walk for when your child can take a stroller nap.

KID-FRIENDLY ATTRACTIONS

Tailor your itinerary to include baby-friendly attractions. The Luxembourg Gardens, for example, offers a tranquil space for kids to play and parents to relax. Many museums offer activities and areas dedicated to young visitors.

DINING OUT

Many Parisian restaurants are small and may not have high chairs available. Dining earlier can help you avoid the busiest times and ensure a more relaxed meal. Bakeries and outdoor food markets are great for picking up quick, kid-friendly meals. We like swinging by Monop' to get freshly squeezed orange juice and snacks to have in our hotel room.

BE FLEXIBLE

Probably the most important tip is to maintain flexibility. With a baby or toddler, it's important to take things at a slower pace and remain adaptable. Your itinerary might change, and that's perfectly fine.

Free
THINGS TO DO IN PARIS

for families

Paris is a city brimming with culture, history, and beauty. It offers plenty of free activities for families. Here are some options that are perfect for families watching their budget.

EXPLORE THE PARKS & GARDENS

Paris is home to beautiful parks and gardens like the Luxembourg Gardens, Tuileries Garden, and Parc des Buttes-Chaumont, where families can picnic, play, or just relax.

VISIT FREE MUSEUMS

On the first Sunday of each month, many of Paris's museums offer free admission, including the Musée d'Art Moderne and the Musée de l'Orangerie (check current policies as they can change).

VISIT NOTRE-DAME CATHEDRAL

While the interior may be under restoration (re-opening is slated for the end of 2024), the exterior of this iconic cathedral remains a breathtaking sight. The surrounding area, including the Seine River banks, offers a picturesque stroll.

STROLL ALONG THE SEINE RIVER

Paris is home to beautiful parks and gardens like the Luxembourg Gardens, Tuileries Garden, and Parc des Buttes-Chaumont, where families can picnic, play, or just relax. The Seine is great for people-watching.

ENJOY STREET PERFORMANCES

Areas like Montmartre, near Sacré-Cœur, often have street performers and artists, offering a glimpse into Paris's artistic soul.

EXPLORE THE MONTMARTRE DISTRICT

Speaking of Montmartre, wandering through its charming streets, exploring the Place du Tertre, and seeing the city from the steps of Sacré-Cœur are all free and memorable experiences.

DISCOVER THE PARC DE LA VILLETTE

This cultural park in the 19th arrondissement hosts free exhibitions and open-air cinema events during summer. It also has several thematic gardens and playgrounds for children.

WATCH THE EIFFEL TOWER SPARKLE

No visit to Paris is complete without seeing the Eiffel Tower's nightly light show, sparkling every hour on the hour after dusk, best viewed from the Trocadéro Gardens.

FREE WORKSHOPS AT ATELIERS DES PETITS

Some cultural centers and libraries in Paris offer free workshops and activities for children, encouraging creativity and learning.

Art Museums

Louvre Museum

While known for its vast and impressive collection, including the Mona Lisa and the Venus de Milo, the Louvre also offers themed visitor trails and workshops designed for families, making exploring art both fun and educational.

📍 93 Rue de Rivoli. 75001 Paris

📞 33 1 40 20 53 17

Musée d'Orsay

Specializing in French art from 1848 to 1914, including masterpieces by Monet, Van Gogh, and Degas, the Musée d'Orsay provides activity booklets for children to help them engage with the art in a fun and interactive way.

📍 Esplanade Valéry Giscard d'Estaing, 75007 Paris

📞 33 1 40 49 48 14

Centre Pompidou

This museum houses a significant modern and contemporary art collection. It's particularly family-friendly thanks to its dedicated children's gallery, Galerie des Enfants, and interactive workshops encouraging creativity and exploration.

📍 Place Georges-Pompidou, 75004 Paris

📞 33 1 44 78 12 33

Musée de l'Orangerie

Known for housing Monet's Water Lilies murals in two oval rooms, the Musée de l'Orangerie is a more intimate museum experience. It often hosts family workshops and guided tours introducing children to Impressionist and Post-Impressionist art.

📍 Jardin des Tuileries, 75001 Paris

📞 33 1 44 50 43 00

Monuments

Paris, a city brimming with history, culture, and beauty, offers countless attractions for families to explore. Here are a few must-see Paris monuments that are particularly engaging for both kids and adults, making them perfect additions to any family trip itinerary.

Eiffel Tower

No visit to Paris is complete without seeing its most iconic landmark. Families can marvel at the tower from the ground, or for a memorable experience, take an elevator ride up to the observation decks for stunning views of the city. The Eiffel Tower's sparkling lights at night are a magical sight that delights visitors of all ages.

Notre-Dame Cathedral

While it is currently under restoration due to the devastating fire in 2019, the majestic Notre-Dame Cathedral remains a breathtaking sight from the outside. Its Gothic architecture, detailed façade, and the history it represents make it a fascinating monument for families to admire.

Montmartre and the Sacré-Cœur Basilica

The winding streets of Montmartre lead up to the stunning Sacré-Cœur Basilica, perched atop a hill overlooking Paris. Families can enjoy the scenic views, explore the artists' square (Place du Tertre), and savor the bohemian atmosphere of this historic neighborhood.

Arc de Triomphe and the Champs-Élysées

Climbing to the top of the Arc de Triomphe offers another unique vantage point of Paris, with panoramic views down the famous Champs-Élysées. The monument, which honors those who fought and died for France, provides a powerful history lesson for older children.

Amazing Kid-Friendly Tours

We usually find the best Paris tours by checking Viator, Get Your Guide, With Locals, and Airbnb Experiences. Always check the company's ratings and reviews to make sure it's the best fit for your family.

Scavenger Hunt at the Musee d'Orsay

This was the BEST tour of Paris we've done as a family! Our guide Caroline was a former elementary school teacher and she basically became a private art history tour for our kids for 2 hours at the Musee d'Orsay. There were hands-on activities and we all learned a lot.

Scavenger Hunt at the Louvre

While we haven't personally done this one, it's also run by Caroline and she does a very similar tour as Musee d'Orsay, except it's at the Louvre. My kids are begging to do this one.

Paris Food Tour

When we travel, we always want to know where to eat. So, that's why we usually book a food tour. There are tons of food tours to choose from in Paris.

Paris Greeters Walk

While I would normally call this a tour, it's technically a volunteer-led "walk" through a neighborhood in Paris as opposed to an official tour. And it's completely free. You'll meet up with a local who will show you around town in an authentic way.

Unexpected Gossip Tour of Paris

Are you ever curious about the people who shaped history but don't really get credit for it? We had the best time on this Paris history tour. Our guide was dressed up in the latest 1700s fashion and told our kids she was a time traveler! She told us all the historical things you don't usually read in textbooks.

Tootbus

If you're looking for a hop-on hop-off bus tour, the Tootbus is great for kids. They have audio guides available in a bunch of different languages and they even have a kids' version.

Paris by Tuk Tuk

You can ride around Paris in an electric TukTuk with your own guide. They have a bunch of different routes you can book. We love that you can get places that are harder to visit with a normal car. Plus, it's pretty unique!

Eiffel Tower Summit Access Group Tour

We pre-booked skip-the-line Eiffel Tower tickets that included a group tour as well as summit access. This is a must-do when traveling to Paris with kids. While a guided tour isn't technically necessary, our guide played a game with the kids that helped pass the time we were waiting for elevators.

Julia Child Food Tour

If you are a fan of the famous chef Julia Child, you'll know that she lived in Paris for a few years and that's where she really learned French cooking. And you'll definitely want to take this Paris food tour!

Giverny and Versailles Day Tour

So, I'm listing this tour last only because it's a super long day and might not work for all families. Personally, we thought it provided a lot of value for our family. It's a 10-hour bus tour that leaves Paris and takes you to Giverny (Monet's home and garden), lunch in the countryside, and the Palace of Versailles before returning back to Paris.

Family Photo Shoot

A family photo shoot is one of our favorite things to do in Paris. I'm serious. The whole family gets a kick out of them, and they usually end up being fun activities.

We set aside a few hours to get the whole family cleaned up and "camera ready." Then we go to a pretty location with our photographer, who makes us feel like total celebrities.

It really takes the pressure off of taking "nice" family photos throughout the trip. We usually print them out to hang on our wall, use them for holiday card photos, add them as our iPhone backdrop, put them in photo books, and share them on social media.

It's really easy to set up a photoshoot in Paris. We've done it three times with Flytographer, a concierge photography website. You just type in that you're looking for photographers in Paris, and it will show you several options. You can look at their portfolios and pick the one you like best. Then, the concierge will sort out all the details. It's one of the most affordable ways to get professional photos in Paris. We've even gotten our photos back before the end of our trip, which is a pretty amazing service.

How to Book Eiffel Tower Tickets

Book in Advance

Eiffel Tower tickets can sell out quickly, especially during peak tourist seasons. To avoid disappointment, book your tickets well in advance. Online booking is available.

The most iconic Paris attraction is the Eiffel Tower, but it can be overwhelming to get tickets (especially during peak seasons). Here are a few things to know:

Choose the Right Ticket Type

There are various ticket options, including tickets to the second floor (via stairs or elevator) and tickets to the summit. Consider your family's comfort and interest level when choosing. I recommend getting skip-the-line tickets, especially during summer months. Remember, children under 4 years old enter for free but still require a ticket.

Consider Time and Day

Try to book your tickets for the morning to beat the crowds or later in the evening to enjoy the sunset and the tower's illumination. Weekdays are generally less crowded than weekends.

Emily in Paris

HOW TO SEE HER USUAL HAUNTS

If your family loves watching "Emily in Paris," visiting Paris offers the exciting chance to see where Emily's adventures happen! One cool spot is the Panthéeon-Sorbonne University, where Emily takes French classes. It's a big, beautiful building that's really old and famous in Paris. Another must-see is the Palais Garnier, the grand opera house where Emily goes to a ballet. It's super fancy and looks like a palace for music and dance!

Emily often hangs out at Place de l'Estrapade, a small square in the Latin Quarter where her apartment and favorite bakery are located. This area is really charming, with lots of cute shops and cafes to explore. Don't forget to visit the Jardin du Palais Royal, a peaceful garden surrounded by cool black and white striped columns where Emily has photo shoots.

For fans of the show, walking around these places can feel like stepping into Emily's world. You might not bump into Emily, but you'll see why she loves Paris so much. Plus, it's a fun way for the whole family to see some beautiful parts of the city that you might not find in every guidebook.

Paris Olympics

Get ready for an unforgettable adventure at the 2024 Paris Olympics from July 26 to August 11! Imagine watching thrilling sports like fencing at the Grand Palais or beach volleyball near the Eiffel Tower. Events will happen all over Paris and even across France in cities like Bordeaux and Lyon, with surfing in Tahiti! The opening ceremony will be a spectacular parade of athletes on boats along the Seine River, ending at the Eiffel Tower. Although it's ticketed, don't worry; there will be 25 free fan zones across Paris, like the Champions Park at Trocadéro, where you can catch the action on giant screens and celebrate the athletes. It's a once-in-a-lifetime chance to enjoy sports and explore Paris with your family!

Paris Day Trips

While there are tons of cool things to do in Paris, it's also worth getting out of the city. Here are the top three day trips from Paris that families often find worth doing, each offering unique attractions and activities suitable for all ages.

Versailles

The Palace of Versailles is a breathtakingly beautiful and historically significant site that's just a short train ride from Paris. Families can explore the opulent palace, marvel at the Hall of Mirrors, and wander through the extensive and immaculate gardens. The estate also features the Trianon Palaces and the Queen's Hamlet, which are less crowded and fascinating for kids to explore. Versailles offers a glimpse into the lavish life of French royalty and provides ample space for kids to run and play outdoors. You can even rent golf carts to zip around the estate.

Giverny

Best known for Claude Monet's house and gardens, Giverny is a peaceful and picturesque day trip option, especially appealing to families interested in art and nature. The colorful gardens, including the famous water lily pond, are wonderfully relaxing and inspirational. Children can appreciate the beauty of the gardens and explore the quaint village of Giverny. Though it's a more laid-back experience compared to Versailles and Disneyland, it offers a chance to immerse in the world that inspired some of Monet's most famous paintings. I highly recommend this for late spring, summer, and early fall.

Disneyland Paris

DISNEYLAND PARIS

DAY TRIP FROM PARIS

You can either take the train or book transportation with your tickets. The key is to do your research before you go to maximize your day. I suggest getting park hopper tickets and splurging for the Disney Premier Access. This is basically their version of Genie Plus and it will save you time. If you've been to Disneyland in California or Walt Disney World in Florida, I'd prioritize attractions you can only find at Disneyland Paris, such as La Tanière du Dragon, Phantom Manor, and The Curious Labyrinth.

MULTI-DAY STAY

If you want to extend your trip, it's nice to spend 2-3 days at the parks. There are lots of Disney hotels within walking distance of the park entrances. This makes it convenient to stay for a few nights.

With longer in the parks, you can get away with just a 1 park per day ticket and take your time to enjoy both new rides and Disney favorites. Plus you'll be able to enjoy all the shows, parades, and character meet-and-greets.

There's also the Disney Village (their version of Disney Springs or Downtown Disney) with tons of shops and restaurants.

Disneyland Hotels

DISNEYLAND HOTEL

Stay like royalty in this 5-star hotel right at Disneyland's entrance, with special park access and surprise shows by Disney characters and performers. It was recently renovated and it's gorgeous.

DISNEY SEQUOIA LODGE

Enjoy a cozy forest getaway inspired by American National Parks, with Bambi-themed rooms and a short 15-minute walk to Disney Parks, all surrounded by beautiful trees near Lake Disney.

DISNEY NEWPORT BAY CLUB

Sail into a 4-star adventure at Disney Newport Bay Club, with its lighthouse guiding you to relaxed elegance, Mickey & Minnie themes, and nautical rooms, all a 15-minute walk from the parks and by Lake Disney.

DISNEY HOTEL NEW YORK - THE ART OF MARVEL

Stay in style at this newly-renovated 4-star hotel with Manhattan vibes. It has over 350 Super Hero artworks, indoor and outdoor pools, a kid's pool, hot tub, and awesome New York theme.

Travel Planner

Travel Budget

TRIP DATES: **NOTES:**

ACCOMMODATIONS	BUDGET	ACTUAL

TRANSPORT & ACTIVITIES	BUDGET	ACTUAL

FOOD & DRINK	BUDGET	ACTUAL

Copy and print this page to keep track of your expenses as you plan your trip.

Travel Checklist

BEFORE YOUR TRIP

Set Alerts for Google Flights
Book Flights and/or Train Tickets
Book Hotel or Rental Home
Try on all clothes before packing
Book Flytographer Photoshoot
Download Paris apps for trip
Make restaurant reservations
Buy tickets for paid tours and activities
Reserve skip-the-line Eiffel Tower
tickets

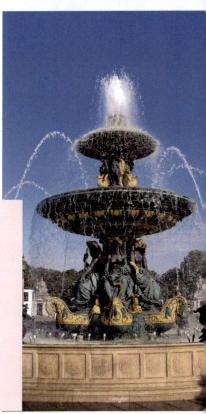

AFTER YOUR TRIP

Receive your Flytographer digital photos
Leave reviews for any businesses
that wowed you
Double-check your credit card(s)
for mistakes or fraudulent charges
Start planning your next trip with
marcieinmommyland.com

Packing List

CLOTHING

- Jacket (winter)
- T-shirts and tank tops
- Long-sleeved shirts
- Sweaters
- Pants and shorts
- Socks and underwear
- Pajamas
- Sunglasses
- Scarf
- Hat
- Dresses
- Swimsuit
- Sandals
- Walking shoes

TOILETRY

- Toothbrush & toothpaste
- Hairbrush & hair ties
- Deodorant
- Shampoo & conditioner
- Hair products
- Sunscreen
- Makeup
- Face wash
- Face lotion
- Eye drops

TECHNOLOGY

- Phone
- Charger(s)
- Laptop, iPad
- Headphones
- Tripod/Selfie stick
- Adapters

MISCELLANEOUS

- Passport (if needed)
- Driver's license
- Cash and credit card
- Travel pillow
- Eye mask
- Earplugs
- Reusable water bottle
- Vitamins
- Prescriptions
- Cold medicines
- First Aid kit
- Hand sanitizer

Apps to Download

PARIS BY METRO

This app is perfect for navigating the Paris Metro system. It helps you plan your route, provides real-time schedules, and even suggests the best ticket options for your trip. This is a must-download.

UBER

For those times when you prefer a car ride to public transportation, Uber is a reliable option in Paris. It's especially handy for traveling with kids when you need a direct route to your destination without the crowds.

GOOGLE MAPS

An essential app for navigating any city, Google Maps is invaluable for finding your way around Paris. It offers directions for walking, public transportation, and driving, as well as information on attractions, restaurants, and more.

PARIS TAXI APP (G7 TAXI)

The official app for Paris's largest taxi network, G7 Taxi, lets you book a taxi instantly or in advance. It's a great option for families who need a car seat, as you can request one through the app. This was our go-to app when there was a Metro strike.

THE FORK

Finding kid-friendly restaurants can be a challenge, but The Fork makes it easier by letting you browse, read reviews, check out menus, and book tables at thousands of restaurants in Paris, often with discounts.

FLUSH - TOILET FINDER

When traveling with kids, knowing where to find the nearest restroom is crucial. Flush helps you locate public toilets around Paris, including information on accessibility and whether a fee is required. You'll want to download this.

Getting around Paris

Arriving in Paris

You'll probably arrive in Paris either via plane or train. Personally, I think it's easies to grab a taxi when you have a bunch of luggage and kids, but there's also an option to use the RER.

CHARLES DE GAULLE AIRPORT

- Airport code: CDG
- Miles from city center: 23 miles
- Transportation options: Uber, Taxi, private transfer, or RER B line

GARD DU NORD

- Miles from city center: 3.5 miles
- Transportation options: Uber, Taxi, private transfer, or RER B line

Using the Paris Metro & RER

Traveling around Paris with your family is super easy thanks to the Paris Metro and RER trains! Here's what you need to know:

CHARLES DE GAULLE AIRPORT

- Airport code: CDG
- Miles from city center: 23 miles
- Transportation options: Uber, Taxi, private transfer, or RER B line

GARD DU NORD

- Miles from city center: 3.5 miles
- Transportation options: Uber, Taxi, private transfer, or RER B line

Navigating Charles de Gaulle

AIRPORT

FAMILY SERVICES

CDG offers various family-friendly services, including play areas located in several terminals, which are great spots for kids to burn off energy after a flight..

NURSING ROOMS

For parents traveling with infants, there are nursing rooms equipped for feeding and changing diapers, providing a private and comfortable space.

STROLLER ACCESSIBILITY

The airport is equipped with elevators and ramps, making it accessible for strollers. However, be prepared for some walking, as the airport is large and terminals can be far apart.

LUGGAGE CARTS

Available throughout the airport, luggage carts can be a huge help. They're free to use and can accommodate bags, making it easier to manage your belongings and keep an eye on your kids.

TRANSPORTATION TO THE CITY

Consider your options for getting to Paris from CDG. The RER B train is efficient but can be challenging with a lot of luggage and small children. Taxis offer a flat rate to the city and may be more convenient for families, and they are available at the taxi ranks outside the terminal. Pre-booking a private transfer can also offer a hassle-free solution directly to your accommodation.

ARRIVAL TIME

Allow for extra time upon arrival for passport control, especially during peak travel seasons. The lines can be long, and with children, it's best to account for delays.

SAFETY AND COMFORT

Keep your family's passports, travel documents, and essentials like snacks, water, and entertainment for the kids easily accessible. Dress your children in comfortable clothes and consider layering, as temperatures in the airport can vary.

Sample
Itinerary

Day 1

ITINERARY

Keep in mind that if you have younger kids, you might just want to plan on morning activities and then go back to your hotel to rest before dinner.

Morning

Paris Food Tour in the Marais District

We all know that Paris is famous for its food. Find out exactly where to go to taste the best croissants. Your guide will take you to famous bakeries where we tried flaky croissants, pastries, and world-renowned bread.

Afternoon

Notre Dame de Paris

The food tour ends fairly close to Notre Dame Cathedral, so walk past it and take a few photos.

Jardin du Luxembourg

This is our favorite park in Paris. You'll find a great playground and lots of areas to run around or enjoy a picnic. Renting toy boats is super popular during the warmer months.

Evening

Dinner Near Your Hotel

After walking around a lot today, you'll probably want to eat somewhere close to your hotel so you can go back and crash.

Day 2

Morning

Flytographer Photoshoot

One of my favorite things to do when traveling with my family is book a photoshoot. That way, I know I'll get some "nice" photos of myself, my kids, and my husband. Otherwise, I'll only be in selfies. And it's great to get it out of the way early in the trip.

Breakfast at Laduree on the Champs Elysees

If you love macarons, chances are that you have heard of Laduree. While you can find their macaron shops all across the world, this location has a full-service cafe and it's gorgeous.

Shopping on the Champs Elysees

The Champs Elysees is one of the most famous shopping streets in Paris. Monoprix and the Disney Store are fun places to pop in with kids.

Day 2

Afternoon

Unexpected Gossip Tour of Paris

Your guide will be dressed in 1700s attire and will spill the tea on all the royal gossip from back in the day. It's a fun way to learn about French history and culture.

Take a Break

At this point, you'll probably want to head back to your hotel to rest. Another option is to head to a park and let everyone zone out for a bit.

Evening

Paris Tootbus

If you're still jet-lagged or want to orient yourself with the city a bit more, hop on the Tootbus. They have audio tours (including a kid-friendly version) and you can rest your legs while still seeing the city.

Galeries Lafayette

Get off the Tootbus near Galeries Lafayette. It's basically a massive department store, but they have a whole section for food. It's a great place to pick up items for a picnic dinner to eat outside. We recommend going to Jardin du Luxembourg.

Day 3

Morning

Scavenger Hunt at the Musee d'Orsay

After a quick breakfast at your hotel, head to the Musee d'Orsay to meet your guide for a kid-focused scavenger hunt of the Musee d'Orsay.

Afternoon

Walk or Take a TukTuk to the Eiffel Tower

Grab lunch at one of the many cafes near the Eiffel Tower. Then meet up for a guided tour of the Eiffel Tower with skip-the-line tickets and Summit Level access.

You can grab cold drinks, ice cream, or crepes afterward and enjoy the view of the Eiffel Tower.

Evening

Dinner at Chez Andres

Make a reservation for Chez Andres. This is a great place to try authentic French cuisine in a comfortable atmosphere. They have a good kids menu and it's a family-friendly restaurant.

Day 4

Morning

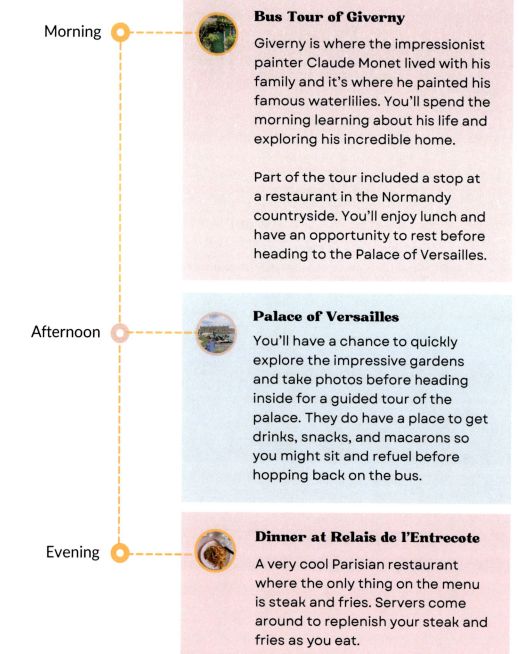

Bus Tour of Giverny

Giverny is where the impressionist painter Claude Monet lived with his family and it's where he painted his famous waterlilies. You'll spend the morning learning about his life and exploring his incredible home.

Part of the tour included a stop at a restaurant in the Normandy countryside. You'll enjoy lunch and have an opportunity to rest before heading to the Palace of Versailles.

Afternoon

Palace of Versailles

You'll have a chance to quickly explore the impressive gardens and take photos before heading inside for a guided tour of the palace. They do have a place to get drinks, snacks, and macarons so you might sit and refuel before hopping back on the bus.

Evening

Dinner at Relais de l'Entrecote

A very cool Parisian restaurant where the only thing on the menu is steak and fries. Servers come around to replenish your steak and fries as you eat.

Day 5

Morning

Disneyland Paris

Grab an early train to Disneyland Paris! It's just about an hour from central Paris and it makes an easy day trip.

Head to Disneyland Park first and knock out your top rides, eat some snacks, and meet some characters.

Afternoon

Decide if you want to eat lunch at Disneyland Park or head across to Wat Disney Studios. Then spend the rest of the afternoon and evening doing rides, seeing shows, and meting characters at Walt Disney Studios.

Evening

After dinner, you'll want to take the train back to your hotel. How late you stay in the parks totally depends on your energy level!

Travel
Resources

Children's Books Set in Paris

- "Madeline" by Ludwig Bemelmans
- "Anatole" by Eve Titus
- "The Invention of Hugo Cabret" by Brian Selznick
- "The Family Under the Bridge" by Natalie Savage Carlson
- "Adele & Simon" by Barbara McClintock
- "Everybody Bonjours!" by Leslie Kimmelman
- "This is Paris" by Miroslav Sasek
- "Linnea in Monet's Garden" by Christina Björk and Lena Anderson
- "Dodsworth in Paris" by Tim Egan
- "Charlotte in Paris" by Joan MacPhail Knight
- "Henri's Walk to Paris" by Leonore Klein and Saul Bass
- "Kiki and Coco in Paris" by Nina Gruener
- "Gustave Eiffel's Spectacular Idea: The Eiffel Tower" by Sharon Katz Cooper
- "Ollie & Moon in Paris" by Diane Kredensor
- "Paris Hop!" by Margie Blumberg
- "Escargot" by Dashka Slater
- "Babar's Guide to Paris" by Laurent de Brunhoff
- "The Mystery of the Mona Lisa: Jack & the Geniuses Book #3" by Bill Nye and Gregory Mone
- "The Red Balloon" by Albert Lamorisse
- "Paris-Chien: Adventures of an Expat Dog" by Jackie Clark Mancuso

Paris Watchlist

Kid TV Shows

- [ ] "Miraculous: Tales of Ladybug & Cat Noir"
- [ ] "The New Adventures of Madeline"
- [ ] "Gaspard and Lisa"
- [ ] "Zak Storm"
- [ ] "Django & Juliette"
- [ ] "Find Me in Paris"
- [ ] "Les Aventures de Tintin"
- [ ] "Trotro"

Kids Movies

- [ ] "Ratatouille" (2007)
- [ ] "The Aristocats" (1970)
- [ ] "Hugo" (2011)
- [ ] "Madeline" (1998)
- [ ] "An American Tail" (1986)
- [ ] "Dilili in Paris" (2018)
- [ ] "The Hunchback of Notre Dame" (1996)
- [ ] "Phantom Boy" (2015)

Grown-Up TV Shows

- [ ] "Emily in Paris"
- [ ] "Call My Agent!" ("Dix pour cent")
- [ ] "The Hook Up Plan" ("Plan Coeur")
- [ ] "Versailles"
- [ ] "Marseille"
- [ ] "Spiral" ("Engrenages")
- [ ] "Lupin"
- [ ] "The Eddy"

Grown-Up Movies

- [ ] "Amélie" (2001)
- [ ] "Midnight in Paris" (2011)
- [ ] "La La Land" (2016)
- [ ] "Before Sunset" (2004)
- [ ] "Paris, je t'aime" (2006)
- [ ] "Moulin Rouge!" (2001)
- [ ] "The Da Vinci Code" (2006)
- [ ] "An American in Paris" (1951)
- [ ] "The Intouchables" (2011)

French Words to Know

Visiting Paris with your family is an exciting adventure, and knowing some basic French phrases can help make things go smoother. Here are the top French words and phrases that parents and families should know for their trip:

- **Bonjour (bon-zhoor)-** Hello. A polite way to greet everyone you meet.
- **Au revoir (oh ruh-vwahr) -** Goodbye. Use this when leaving a place or saying goodbye to someone.
- **Merci (mehr-see) -** Thank you. Essential for showing gratitude.
- **S'il vous plaît (seel voo pleh) -** Please. It's important to be polite when asking for something.
- **Où est...? (oo eh...?) -** Where is...? Useful for finding places, like **"Où est la toilette?"** (Where is the bathroom?).
- **Pardon/Excusez-moi (par-dohn/ex-kew-zay mwah) -** Excuse me. For getting attention, apologizing, or making your way through a crowd.
- **Combien ça coûte? (kohm-byen sah koot?) -** How much does it cost? Important for shopping and activities.
- **L'addition, s'il vous plaît (la-dee-syon, seel voo pleh) -** The check, please. For when you're finished dining at a restaurant.
- **Je voudrais... (zhuh voo-dray...) -** I would like... Perfect for ordering food or making a polite request.
- **Aidez-moi, s'il vous plaît (ehd-mwah, seel voo pleh) -** Help me, please. In case you need assistance.

- **Non merci (non mehr-see) -** No thank you. Useful for declining offers politely.
- **C'est combien? (say kohm-byen?) -** How much is it? Another way to ask the price of something.
- **Je ne comprends pas (zhuh nuh kom-prahn pah) -** I don't understand. For when you need clarification.
- **Parlez-vous anglais? (par-lay voo ahn-glay?) -** Do you speak English? Handy if you're struggling with French and need someone who speaks English.
- **Je suis désolé(e) (zhuh swee day-zo-lay) -** I'm sorry. For men, it's **"désolé,"** and for women, **"désolée"** with an extra "e" at the end.
- **Oui (wee) -** Yes. Simple but essential for responding affirmatively.
- **Non (nohn) -** No. Just as important for expressing disagreement or declining something.
- **Je cherche... (zhuh shairsh...) -** I'm looking for... Helpful when searching for specific places or items.
- **Pouvez-vous m'aider? (poo-vay voo meh-day?) -** Can you help me? When you need assistance.
- **Où sont les toilettes? (oo sohn lay twa-let?) -** Where are the bathrooms? Essential for families with young children.

These phrases cover basic interactions and needs while exploring Paris, making your family trip smoother and more enjoyable. Don't worry about perfect pronunciation; locals appreciate any effort to speak their language!

DOWNLOAD

This entire guide is available as an interactive digital PDF that you can download onto your phone and carry around with you on your trip. It's the easiest way to see exactly which tours/attractions I recommend and get the best deals.

Free Digital Guide

Use the QR code above and enter

PARISWITHKIDS

as the coupon code at check out to access your free digital copy.

@marcieinmommyland

FIND MORE INSPIRATION FOR YOUR PARIS TRIP!

Join my email list to keep up with the latest Paris tips, attractions, tours, and other kid-friendly destinations worldwide, only on marcieinmommyland.com.

Made in the USA
Las Vegas, NV
13 July 2024

92261196R00050